clairvoyant giving

both face to face ar

She was heard as the psychic astrologer, "Madam Debra", on the Danny Greenstone Radio Show on BBC Three Counties Radio from 2008/9 and revived this role on Jnet Radio. She is also the author of "The Twin Soul Connection" which appeared in Soul and Spirit magazine, "The Twin Soul Waiting Room", "The Physiology of Love at First Sight – A Karmic Re-Sit in 'Amour'" "Time Portals" and other articles, plays and sketches.

Debbie formed D&D Psychic Events with her cousin Diane in 2009.

Together they appear at private parties and fayres and are available for bookings for hen nights, birthday parties, bar mitzvahs and any other kind of function.

www.debbienagioff.co.uk

debbiemaya@yahoo.co.uk

The Twin Flame and other Soul Mate Connections

By Debbie Nagioff

Biography

Debbie Nagioff is an internationally renowned clairvoyant, with a specialist field in reading the energies surrounding soul mate connections, which often leads her to tune into **past lives**.

Debbie also works as a writer, journalist, broadcaster, and astrologer. She gained a diploma at **the** Mayo School of Astrology in 1978. She trained at the College of Psychic Studies in South Kensington and has worked, for over 30 years as a

Forward by Debbie Nagioff

We encounter many soul mates in this life from the time we are born, till the day we die. Mothers, fathers, sisters, brothers, cousins, uncles and aunts, best friends, lovers, husbands, wives. Yet arguably the meeting that has the greatest impact on our lives and our psyche, is that between twin flames (or twin souls). Suffice to say it's a very rare connection indeed.

If I had not experienced such a meeting, I doubt I would have had the necessary credentials to write this book. It took me some years before I realised that this connection or, to be more honest, re-connection, was not just about the friendship and relationship it yielded, and the supportiveness, but it pushed me further along my psychic and creative path to a place where I could help others going through soul trauma, with compassion, empathy, deep understanding and without judgment.

To all those who have suffered the bereavement of soul mate separation and feel they are truly going insane; to those involved in a soul connected relationship they haven't the words to describe or label and are desperate to so to do, this book is for you.

Chapters

1.   The Twin Soul Connection

2.   Different types of soul mates

3.   Case Studies

4.   Soul mates and the past life connection

5.   The pain of separation from the soul mate and how to deal with it in the Twin Soul Waiting Room

6.   Reading the energies, moving forward, advice to the sitter

Chapter 1 – The Twin Soul Connection

I turned round to meet him and as he approached to shake my hand I felt an electrical current run through my veins. Alchemy was at work. A tsunami of feverish emotion and love flooded every part of my being, and though this man was a total stranger to me, there was recognition of a pre-existing passion for him, so deep and so established that it transcended present time and stretched back over many shared lifetimes and forward into eternity.

As a working clairvoyant I am endlessly confronted with the entire scale of human misery and joy. One issue I've come across time and time again is the soul mate connection. One can probably discern three different types of Soul mate connections, and **all** of them are karmic.

1. The regular soul mate connection in which we find we connect quite happily and comfortably with someone, with very little effort. We feel we've known them all our life.

2. Next is the real karmic soul mate connection – This can be very hard work. You may have an intense like or dislike for that person, but they come into your life to teach you something. A lesson has to be learned and a debt repaid (not literally money!). This can be extremely painful, but is necessary for our spiritual growth. Once the lesson is learned, the relationship has done its job and we may find we've shifted onto another path.

3. Finally there is the connection that time never dims, the Twin Soul or Twin Flame connection.

Here there is an instant attraction of energies, the energy of the two souls connecting over time, over miles, and sometimes over years. Very often there is an initial meeting of the Twin Souls and often one half of the duo is more spiritually awakened and "gets it". The other may not be quite there, but nevertheless they are deeply touched by the experience.

Sometimes they remain in contact like this, and sometimes the two are "deliberately" torn apart and separated over years to go and work on their own lives and commitments and deal with karma in other relationships before finally reuniting decades down the line.

But are the twin souls destined to be together?

Synchronicity is at work here to bring the two back together again. How entrancing to find the same magical alchemy still at work, just as it was at the first meeting – A recognition of a deep rooted love so entrenched and so accepted, it could only have been forged in other lifetimes together, and probably that is what love at first sight is, recognition of an ancient love.

Inevitably in Twin Soul connections we come up against the "dance" the connection and the disconnection between the two that is incredibly frustrating, and cannot be rushed. We are dealing with a process here. Within the connection you often find that one party is very keen to move the relationship on to higher levels, whilst the other doesn't know what is going on and doesn't want to deal with the relationship. This is because it touches deep and painful emotions that they may have been suppressed and they don't want to deal with. So they try and escape the relationship.

The latter of the pairing is often referred to as the "runner". The intensity of the connection means that each one feels the other's pain and confusion and there is much telepathic interchange. Both are pulled around by the compulsion of the energy, and are connected by what seems like an umbilical cord.

Often one of the pair can't take the heat in the kitchen and runs away and when this happens, the other twin experiences a bereavement, which never heals, until the next reconnection. The "runner" has perhaps experienced a lifetime of destructive love affairs. Unable to accept love when it is proffered (even though they may crave it), they may have trashed it, kicked it around like a football and found subtle ways to push it away. Feelings of unworthiness and claustrophobia are usually at the root here. Or it could be that they have simply never found the right person, until now.

In these circumstances and when used against the other twin, the experience is like a searing pain through the heart. In conventional relationships eventually the wound is healed, but in a Twin Soul connection, the situation only gets worse and worse.

Gripped in mutual "obsessive" behaviour the energy can be confusing especially when the "dance" is in full swing. It is quite common for the "runner" to profess language bordering on "I love you," although this can be well camouflaged and veiled, and then for that "runner" to retract and contradict what they have said. They feel foolish and vulnerable. When a "runner" runs, they run.

But before we return to the twins, let's look at other soul mate connections.

Chapter 2. Different types of soul mates

Yes, but is he a twin soul or not?

One of the first questions that is always proffered before I do a soul connection reading, is, "is he/she my twin soul?" Until I am able to connect into the energies of the sitter or person on the other end of the telephone, it is difficult to tell.

There is only one twin soul connection. By its very nature you can only have one twin. And in nine out of ten cases as I tune into the situation, I can feel what kind of soul mate connection it is, and very seldom is it that kind of relationship. In fact in most cases the relationship is one designed to teach a valuable lesson.

It would be pompous of me to say that if you <u>have</u> to ask the question as to whether you're in a twin soul set up or not, then you're probably not, but twin soul connections tend to happen to people who are already well along their psychic path. The other half of the connection may not be as advanced as you are, or may not comprehend it, but they too have chosen a spiritual way of life.

Ongoing synchronicity, for me is one of the major signs of a twin flame connection. Telepathic thinking is peculiar to many types of soul mate unions, but it's the ongoing synchronicities of life that mark out the twin. The two may have met years before where the connection and feeling of intense love was instantaneous, and the bolt of lightning resembled a plug fitting into a socket in an otherwise darkened room.

The intensity of feeling surpasses more conventional sexual attractions as your soul re-connects with theirs. Kundalini rises, your chakras are buzzing and your life is changed forever. And when you are apart from your twin soul, it feels like bereavement.

Very often the two are torn apart by circumstances, but can meet up in the oddest of situations years down the line, once they have cleared or nearly cleared other karmic connections. There may still be residues of karma left to clear, but the same plug fits easily into the same socket as the years fall away. The intensity of feeling is still there still connected. And it is what it is. Twin soul connections don't follow conventional patterns.

There are other soul mates that we get together with and get along with, without any effort whatsoever. The closeness of good friends which is as comfortable as a pair of old slippers. Nothing needs explaining between the two of you.

Example

A school friend, we shall call her Jan, meeting someone destined to be one of their best friends for a lifetime at 14 years old commented, "I think you and I are going to be friends for a long time". The connection was as if they'd known each other a lifetime already, yet maybe had only met an hour before. Their energies were in sync and they had spent other lifetimes together.

Similarly soul connections can be with people we detest, but nevertheless their importance in your life is to move you on to another path or teach you a lesion.

Example

'Suzie', was working for many years as a legal secretary. She was superficially happy in her work, but unfulfilled and she knew it. But nevertheless the people in the office were very pleasant, the salary was extremely useful for paying the bills and there was a balance in her life. But then came a change. Suzie moved in to her boyfriend's house so her usual easy train journey into work became protracted. Suzie had to walk to the station, travel several miles and then change again, only to make a further change.

She became tired and irritable. But then there was a further problem. Her company suddenly, and without consulting her, brought in a woman to be her direct line manager.

This woman's job was to basically spy on her to see if she was doing her work correctly and to check how often she used the phone. In essence she became an exhibit in a goldfish bowl. This provoked Suzie to not only complain bitterly, but to take the matter further. There were blazing rows, personnel got involved, the partners in the firm, who'd prefer to turn a blind eye, couldn't. And all along what Suzie wanted to do was do tarot readings. A friend asked her why she carried on taking this matter further and further and higher and higher. Suzie had been conditioned by her mother to hang on to a job, any job, but she was now a divorced mother of 55. Why was she still living by those rules. Her own home had been rented out, she didn't need to work under these conditions. It was humiliating. And yet still she stayed till eventually she made herself ill.

Once more this friend intervened and asked her why she stayed and made herself ill – Suzie had no answer to give. And so, with great courage she finally handed in her notice and continued to build up a very successful tarot reading business. Fate had brought into her life a difficult soul mate connection, guaranteed to get the hackles on her neck to stand up. But it was in fact just what she needed to move her on to the right path.

No-one leaves a cheerful set up. It's only when things become difficult and intolerable that they are compelled to change and move on. And Madam Destiny brings into our lives these difficult characters in order to, ultimately, help us find our way.

Chapter 3. Case Studies

Sometimes I have the strangest feeling about you. Especially when you are near me as you are now. It feels as though I had a string tied here under my left rib where my heart is, tightly knotted to you in a similar fashion. And when you go to Ireland, with all that distance between us, I am afraid that this cord will be snapped, and I shall bleed inwardly – Edward Rochester – Jane Eyre (Charlotte Bronte)

As a clairvoyant I have met and spoken with many people going through some kind of soul mate trauma, and suffering pain that is no different from that experienced during bereavement.

I have changed names, dates etc. to protect people's privacy, but let them tell their stories.

(i) Janey's Story

I have a soul connection with a man, and he is a runner. I need to know what is going on, what are the lessons in all of this.. What are we both learning? Is he almost ready to face things?

An opportunity has arisen for me to meet up with Phillip, and to be in the same city, but I am facing an inner struggle as to whether I should or should not go.

I believe he will come to me when he is ready. I have this inner dialogue thing going on that says should I go or leave it alone. Oh yes, I forgot to say, he's with a girl called Carol now. So he's moved on. But, if I see him, I think I would fall apart.

I'm just trying to live my life as best as I can and I miss him so much, it hurts.

I learned that Philip and Carol bought a home together. I guess it is really clear that he will not be leaving or they will not be ending as we all had hoped. The physical direction is them getting more and more entrenched in a life together, not coming apart.

Verdict: When I spoke with Janey on the phone, she really was in a desperate way. It was very clear that Philip had run, and Janey was persistent yet distressed, and wanted to know if he would come back. It was clear from my first reading with her that Philip had to fulfil his karmic obligations with Carol, however long that took.

Janey courageously decided to call upon Philip when she was visiting the area on business. She never let on she was coming, and when she did see him, he was extremely cold towards her.

His girlfriend Carol began shouting at Janey, clearly threatened by her appearance. Did Janey do the right thing? What did she learn about the relationship she had with Philip? Maybe it was too much for him to deal with.

Sometimes the lessons we are learning at the time, are too painful to acknowledge.

(ii) <u>Melanie</u>'s Story

I swear I could write a book about my 'soul connection' I just don't have an ending! When I met him it was like something in me just told me he was the one. I can't explain why I thought that. It was just a feeling inside of me. He was a friend of my brother-in-law and wanted me to meet him but I was against it at the time. But we did meet and it was fireworks.

In time he got engaged even though we had this connection and he was struggling with it.

His friends didn't think he should marry this girl, and he ended up doing so anyway. I removed myself from the situation, but then around six months later he contacted me, as the marriage seemed to be on the rocks. She was sleeping with other guys.

We dated and I just felt he was the one, but then he ran. Did I mention he was in the military? Anyhow, he got sent overseas and he ended the relationship. I was in such pain. But the story doesn't end there.

Three years later he came back to me and we starting going together. But it seemed life had changed him. I guess this happens with army guys. They see so much. He couldn't commit to me, and I just had to end it. It broke my heart. But all around me are signs of him, and synchronicity type things. What does it all mean?

Verdict: As I tuned into this situation I really felt that Melanie needed to take a large step back from it. Very often people feel they can control the situation, but it's not so in these instances. I did feel that her army boy would return, but in his own time. She needed to heal, and he was emotionally very scarred from what he had experienced in Afghanistan.

(iii) Jake

I feel my life is in a muddle emotionally, and I just don't know what's going on. And I find that strange, particularly as I'm a middle-aged man! Let me explain.

First is my ex wife, Jan, who I met years ago (1974) at college, and within an hour of meeting her I knew she would be my wife. I was besotted by her, but she only wanted me as a friend.

After a few years we did 'get it together' as they say and lived together - after 7 years I realised that I wasn't happy with Jan (there was friction with my family and life with her was difficult at times). We semi-split up, she insisted that we went to marriage guidance (although not married) who eventually suggested that we should marry - this I tried to resist but Jean was like a steam roller.

Eventually I decided to give it a go and hoped that marriage might make things better - it didn't.

After 20+ years of marriage, our son having left home I was feeling isolated (we had no friends - Jan didn't seem to like anybody) I took to the internet and chatted to people about odds and ends just to have some social contact.

I talked to an American woman 19 years younger than me, Sandy, when she eventually sent her picture I felt that she was maybe the one. She was having problems with her boy friend and our emails talked of our personal problems and became romantic. I felt that I was being a typical old bloke falling for a pretty younger woman. I also realised that I had a lot to lose financially - my business and my house. Sandy and I have never met only email and telephone conversations.

Strangely she once posted a picture of her holding something in the palm of her hand and I felt I recognised her hand - looked like a smaller version of mine.

Through Sandy I learned that my ideas about how a man and woman might live together weren't as stupid as Jan would have me believe. Sandy also wondered if we had chased each other through various lives but had never actually met. Anyway our relation cooled and we spoke less often.

Finally a woman called Donna contacted me via friends reunited as we had been at junior school together, although we had had very little to do with each other. She had left her husband and in many ways was quite determined to take our relationship further. Mind you she was pushing at an open door. I eventually left my wife, moved in with Donna and got a divorce.

Many psychics who have seen us together say that we have a lovely aura around us and that we are soul mates.

I am pretty sure that Donna loves me and I find her easy to be with but have never felt the feeling that she is the one. We are also quite different in some aspects - humour and music, whereas with Jan and Sandy these things were very similar.

Jake wondered if he was with the right woman, and that his wife, Jan wanted him back.

Verdict: I tuned into Jake's chaotic situation and tried to fathom it all out. It's very important that people realise that clairvoyance isn't a fortune-telling tool and when dealing with soul mate connections, I always try and kick start people into thinking and working on their own situations, giving advice, as I am given it via spirit, and then asking them questions about why they are so attracted to the person they are with.

I felt in Jake's case that he just didn't know what he wanted, and I wasn't about to tell him what he needed.

(iv) Eileen

I was engaged when young to Larry for about 4 years. I guess we both felt we wanted space and that there might be something better. They we split up. I then went on to marry someone else, and so did he. My husband and I had an amicable divorce after 20 years or so, and I found myself thinking about Larry again. But we live in different parts of the States, he in Los Angeles, and me in New York and I contacted him via Facebook. There was no response at first, but then we got into a gentle kind of emailing situation.

He's been on my mind 24/7 and although he is married, I've been desperate to see him again, even if it is just as a friend. After much soul-searching I suggested to him that we should meet. I do have family in Los Angeles, and I said to him that I would come and visit. But I still got no response. I was in two minds as to whether to book the flight, but took my courage in my hands and did so. After I booked it, Larry wrote to me and told me his situation. He was desperately sick and didn't know if he would be able to see me or not. I was devastated, but did the trip anyway.

I never did get to see Larry. I was so unhappy and desperate. I emailed him again after I got back and didn't hear from him for some time, but eventually he did get back in contact.

Verdict: I felt Eileen was so desperate to see Larry, obviously, but that she was thinking very much (and naturally so) about herself and not reading the signs about how ill he was. It was as if she wanted to block that situation from her mind. I don't see Larry as the "runner" here, more like Eileen having to learn to consider his feelings. It's a difficult situation when one soul mate is so hell bent on being with the other. The lesson here is always about unconditional love and taking a step back to read the signs.

(v) Irene

I saw a clairvoyant last year and they told me I had met my twin flame which would be great but the person in question is breaking my heart. Currently the situation is driving me crazy.

ght I looked up what the twin connection was about and came across an article which described the feelings of such a connection. It explained how you feel - you know this person from the moment you meet them, cannot stop thinking about them, come together, break apart, then meet again quite by accident and go through all sorts of torment and pain even though from a practical point of view the situation is all wrong.

At the same time you know you cannot walk away and if you did you would just be haunted forever by them. Does this make sense or am I just crazy?

Verdict: When I read for Irene I knew there was something that had been left out of the story. As I tuned into the energies surrounding this soul connection, it was obvious to me that the man who she was infatuated with was playing her for a fool. No matter how much she said this was a twin flame, and I didn't doubt that it was a soul connection, it didn't feel right. She had met this man through work. She was in a high powered job, his company was offering services to hers.

They met and there was an instant sexual attraction. But as I tuned in, I felt he was playing her. She had been very cool about it, but she had a great passion for him, but there was something else. She had loaned him a very large sum of money, and he hadn't repaid it. She'd left it and left it, and finally asked him when he would pay her back. He couldn't. She ended up suing him, but loving him at the same time.

If there was every a karmic pay back in every sense of the word, Irene's situation embraced it. Clearly a lesson to be learned here.

(vi) Christine

I've been very happily married living in Europe. I'm from New York originally, and am in a very well paid job in London. I was sent on a course from work and met a guy who has been travelling for some time. I just can't get him out of my head and he is on my mind 24/7. But I am still very happily married and can't understand why I feel like this.

Verdict: In my experience deep soul connections usually happen when they are supposed to happen, and not always at convenient times. Christine's meeting with Jake, through her into total confusion. Yet, all along she said her relationship with her husband, John, was fantastic. As I tuned in further I could see that

Christine's early life experience of divorced parents had made her determined to have the perfect marriage. I didn't doubt that her husband was all that she said he was. But Jake represented danger and excitement, and it was those elements that were missing from her perfect set up.

So why had he been brought into her life, now? This, I felt was a test of strength for her. A test to look at her situation with honesty, but not necessarily to tear her marriage apart.

(vii) Emma-Sue

Among the many situations I have read, this was the most disturbing, although I always read without judgment. I shall let Emma-Sue tell her story.

I come from a very religious background, very respectful, etc., but in an effort to understand why my daughter was dating a man I found sexually deviant (I say this because he had actually made a pass at me!), I decided to go on line and enter a chat room, posing as a 22 year old. My daughter is 22 and I am 45. I wanted to understand what made her tick.

As I began chatting with various young people, I connected with Jim. We seem to bond very early on, and I would miss our chats when he didn't come on line. Jim was 22 and I always made out that I was a young person in a very heavy relationship that I wanted to get out of. Jim was so involved with me, and I with him, that I just didn't want to break the spell. He used to dream about me, but then I had only showed him pictures of myself when I was very young.

Many times he wanted to meet me, but I always made up some excuse as to why we shouldn't. We live about 1500 miles away from each other.

Finally I came clean and told him the truth, and he backed off so quickly and I haven't heard from him since. I am heart broken.

Verdict: In this situation Emma Sue had been the trickster in every possible way. She had a very controlling husband and she was very unhappy in her marriage. I didn't doubt that the relationship she had made with Jim was a deep one, but built on lies and fabrication. This is deeply shocking from a soul point of view, and is a situation that seems, at this stage, irreparable.

(viii) Helen's story

I am a married woman of 56. When I was 18 (in 1973) I was working for a leading television network in Los Angeles as a secretary, but in one of their technical departments. But I was bored and wanted to do something else. In order to appease me, the network personnel seconded me to another job within the organisation working for the producer of a very well known comedy show at the time.

One of the guys in the department was a writer called Johnnie, and when he walked in the door to meet me, I had a revelation. I fell profoundly in love with him in seconds and distinctly remembered almost jumping back when he shook my hand, such was the electrical energy I felt pass between us.

From that moment on, I couldn't bear to be in the same office as him. I was so afraid my feelings would show.

But then disaster struck and the producer felt I was totally unsuitable for the job, probably because I was rendered useless by this "romantic" event in my life. And so I had to go back to my old job.

After that, I probably saw Johnnie twice more in the 70s, once we met for a drink, and five years later, in 1978, I was seconded to another job in the same building.

Fast forward to the 90s, and I was now living in New York, married to Simon, with two children and working in an entirely different environment. I was working for a fashion magazine a few days a week. But then I bumped into an old friend of mine from my television networking days.

Gary was now some big shot executive producer in television who visited the city frequently. We used to text each other and meet up once a year or see each other around.

I told my husband about him, but little was I to know that Gary would be the catalyst that would bring me back to my twin soul, Johnnie. Actually in those days I didn't know anything about twin souls, but I did have a great interest in the metaphysical, and I also loved writing.

So my life had taken me out of the media, and onwards.

In 2004, Simon and I were talking generally about writers. I mentioned I had worked for Johnnie all those years back. At the time Johnnie lived in San Diego. So it was a shock when Simon said that, not only had he worked with Johnnie (because Johnnie was well known in those days), but that Johnnie had moved to New York and in fact now lived two or three miles away from me. I found this astounding. Of all the places in the States that he could live, and the areas, he was 5 minutes away from me.

I asked Simon if I should send Johnnie any of my work to look at, and he said it would be best if I sent him something that was finalised, rather than anything else. So another nine months elapsed before I did that. I looked his address up and sent him my work, little thinking if it was the right person. About a week later I not only received a very long letter from him, and he had remembered me very well, but also an email.

We then fell into a fairly regular emailing situation. I was very keen to meet up with him, but he never pushed that.

At this stage I guess I felt very curious to know what he looked like. After all, he had been 15 or so years older than me, so he would be quite elderly now. Still, that didn't stop me.

I had to wait another 18 months before fate intervened. My husband is not a great theatre fan, he prefers his sport. He has never interfered with me meeting up with friends of either sex. There was a comedy show on in town.

I texted Simon to see if he wanted to see it. He was very keen because he had worked with the leading actor many years back. I also emailed other friends, and Johnnie who mentioned that he might come along as he had also worked with the leading actor. My heart raced.   But what if he didn't come?

That evening when I arrived at the theatre, Simon texted me to say he would be late and to leave a ticket at the box office, which I duly did.

I sat down in my seat, and looked around the theatre to see if I could see anyone who would resemble Johnnie, but 30 years on. I saw no-one and resigned myself to the fact that he wouldn't come. However, 5 minutes before curtain up, a very distinguished man entered my row, looked at his ticket,   looked   at   me   and announced, "excuse me, but I think you're sitting in my seat". And so I was. I had just plumped myself down on what I thought was my seat, and it was his. We had a brief conversation, but then the lights went down.

Simon arrived 15 minutes later and in the interval and after the show we all got together. When I was talking to Johnnie again, the same feelings of great intensity I felt rising inside me, like a Tsunami wave of karmic recognition and love. I could see something was happening with him too. We agreed to all get together to discuss scripts and writing etc. And more or less from that day forward in

2007 Johnnie and I have emailed each other virtually every day.

Since that time Johnnie and I have got closer, but I know he would do nothing to jeopardise my marriage. He lives alone, having separated from him wife many years ago.

He does have a companion, but their relationship is just that. But with me we are great and loving friends. But like most twin soul connections it is very hard to label this one. We aren't boyfriend and girlfriend, nor are we lovers, nor are we just friends. But the connection has been a roller-coaster. It has only been in the last year or so that I have learned acceptance of its possibilities.

Synchronicity has played a huge role. Even before we met up again and my husband and I were looking to move from our previous house, we actually looked at a house two doors away from where Johnnie lives now.   But then there have been so many coincidences, I have lost count. All I know is that everything that is creative and my own path in life has been truly changed and enhanced with Johnnie in my life.

Verdict: This is truly what twin soul connections are like. A rollercoaster of emotions, sudden re-connections across time and space, endless synchronicity, and a huge dollop of pain and then, hopefully, a movement forward into acceptance.

As you can see soul mates come in all flavours, but one of the main effects of meeting a soul mate that you feel deep love for is that it changes you.

In most of these cases the soul connection was made to effect change and repay a karmic debt. In all these situations, much pain has been experienced and not all, if any of these examples are twin soul connections, but that does not lessen the effect of the lessons that have to be learned, nor does it take away from the feelings that have been felt.

Chapter 4 Soul mates and the past life connection

Just for a moment he shakes her hand.
Just for a moment she catches his eye
Just for a moment he glimpses her soul
Just for a moment they transcend time
By Debbie Nagioff

Love at first sight?

You've walked into a room or you're just about to be introduced to somebody and even before that first "hello" or "please to meet you", wham! You step into a parallel universe, your body is shaking, your heart is singing and the rest of the world melts away?

Many of us have experienced the phenomenon of falling in love at first sight. But physiologically what is going on here? Just think about it. You <u>haven't</u> even met this person yet. They may be walking towards you and smiling, or simply looking across a crowded room at you. How can it be that in that moment we have connected with them at such a deep soul level that we are willing to change our whole life to accommodate them?

But we haven't even shaken hands, and at the moment we do, there is an electrical current, that thunderbolt moment. But what exactly is happening?

Physiologically our chakras (the energy centres in our body) are spinning and buzzing with excitement. Think on it. The solar plexus chakra is humming and saying "don't I remember you from somewhere?"

The heart chakra is swelling and expanding like a budding flower that has lain dormant since winter and has by-passed spring straight into summer. The spleen chakra, let's face it, has it's own pulsating agenda! The throat chakra is literally choking with all these unsung emotions and wants to say "where have you been all this time?"

And can that be the clue? "Where have they been all this time?" In more conventional, though no less important relationships we meet someone, we get to know them, we may feel sexual attraction, a meeting of minds, and whatever and the relationship has a pattern. But in Love at First Sight. Are we dealing with a past life love affair that was not resolved? Why else are we so enraptured so quickly. Here we have a meeting of souls.

Our soul has remembered theirs, but in our current life thought process we think we are meeting them for the first time.

So everything is beautiful. But what we don't realise is that this "meeting" has been metaphysically "arranged" by Madam Destiny in her guise as Chief Examiner and Human Chess Master and you've been given the opportunity to meet up again with this karmic soul and "re-sit" the love test with them and resolve the issues in this life time.

In the cold light of day however, for lesser enlightened souls, they can slip into "Woody Allen" mode. "What am I going to do?" "What's happening to me?" "How can I be falling in love?"

"My Analyst will think me crazy" "My palms are all sweating". "What if I imagined it all?" "What if they don't feel the same?" "I'm going to flunk it".

The last remarks are perhaps the most telling for people. They believe they've imagined it and they're going to be rejected and they enter into a kind of soul-dance with the other person.*

For those souls willing to take this chance again and re-sit "Amour" with this person, the hard work starts here as you slowly begin to discover <u>why</u> you have been brought together again and the obstacles you have to overcome this lifetime.

Chapter 5. The pain of separation from the soul mate and how to deal with it in the Twin Soul Waiting Room

There is often, as I've said before in this book, much pain surrounding the separation of soul mates, a dull ache which never seems to go away, and none more so acute than between twin souls. So how do we deal with that pain and what's it all about.

I am aware that many people who are fixated with another and have some knowledge of soul mate connections, automatically assume that the person monopolising their thoughts 24/7, must be their twin.   In some cases this is true and in other cases it isn't.   But how do we know? I have always stuck resolutely by my own mantra that, if you have to ask another person whether a third party is your twin soul, then the answer is probably no.

My feeling has always been that synchronicity, unusual meetings, unusual re-meetings the intensity and pull of the connection and the seemingly inability to characterise or label the "relationship" (and various other criteria) point towards a twin soul rather than a regular soul mate.

And so you've met your twin soul. You've identified them and know instinctively that they are the other half of your soul. But how do you hurry things along? The answer is you don't.

This can be incredibly frustrating for the more aware soul in that waiting room figuratively reading through countless old magazines waiting eternally for the re-connection, waiting for the other half of their soul to understand and acknowledge the connection. But will they? In my experience the energy pull, which is rather like an electrical chord, works both ways, and the feelings are the same even though as individuals we express ourselves differently from our twin.

In my clairvoyant experience twin souls are continuously challenged before they can finally reunite. Very often one or both are involved in another karmic deal that has to be seen through to the end. That other relationship in itself can delay the timing of the twin souls reuniting. And for that soul in the waiting room it can be the worst kind of emotional pain. Will she/he ever leave that other karmic connection?

In the way of things, twin souls have to experience these separations, it's part of the contract! During these times we learn so much about ourselves and we learn about unconditional love. Knowing that your other half (and this isn't always your spouse or girl/boyfriend) must fulfil their earthly karmic obligations is extremely challenging. It is not a question of being a doormat, or putting your own life on hold. It's about acknowledging this deep love and knowing that your twin soul is <u>always</u> connected to you whatever you might do, and whoever else you may be with.

People who consult me are very keen to know <u>when</u> they will reunite with their twin. That's not always easy to pinpoint. Spirit timing is notoriously icult to ascertain. This is because spirit time is different from earth time. If you imagine spirit are sitting on the upper deck of a London double decker bus, they can see further up the road than us mere mortals. And so frequently they will think an event has already happened, when in fact it hasn't.

Sometimes twin souls have a fleeting meeting very early on. One soul feels it, but the other doesn't have the vocabulary to acknowledge what they've experienced, or indeed may not perceive their other half in the same way. In other words, this early meeting may be an indicator that one or both are not picking up the radar signal.

Many years may elapse before the two meet up again. The energies and the feelings are exactly the same. The knowing twin may feel pangs of regret and anger that their other half did not reunite with them sooner. But the Universal time is usually accurate. Just think, if your twin soul had been in your life all along, but had other karmic relationships to fulfil, that would have been heartbreaking for you.

It could mean that one twin would have not lived a full life, always hoping, always wishing and always waiting, when it was not time to wait, and therefore not become the person they should have been.

Although in some respects there may never been a right time, till the right time arrives, Madam Destiny will eventually have her say!

So what can we learn in that waiting room? We learn not to try and force our will on the other? That type of controlling behaviour is for lesser soul connections to learn the folly of their ways and to learn that unconditional love is not about controlling or bullying the other person.

We learn that as our twin soul gradually comes to understand the connection and feels the love, without fear and without running away, so the two of you will eventually unite in harmony for all eternity.

Chapter 6. Reading the energies, moving forward and advice to the sitter

I always explain to sitters exactly how this business works, according to my thinking. We work on energies, whether it be face to face or on the phone. Clairvoyants use their scrying powers to access the Universal energy pool through their crown chakra. In that way they feel know that some events feel more closer than others.

The energies surrounding more immediate and closer events have an urgency about them. Those that are a year or two away can be felt, but not in the same way. In terms of twin soul re-connections, all we can tell is that this will happen, but not yet.

Whenever we are dealing with soul mate connections especially that of a twin soul, I always tell my "souls" that all this "needfulness" and pain they are experiencing, which is literally tearing them apart, has to be somehow controlled and eased. I always advise taking a step back. You wouldn't walk into a fire by choice, and this flame feels the same. You must step back in order to reassess to heal yourself and take stock of the situation.

In time the pain of the loss will ease, although it never really goes away. But there is life to be lived and whilst your soul connection is still trying to figure out what's happening, in his/her own time, why should you put your own life on hold? Just know that there will come a time when things will be worked through.

My advice always to anyone having a sitting with me, be it a soul mate reading or a general one, is to avoid trying to think or wish too hard for someone particular to come through from spirit to talk to you.

Sometimes they will and sometimes they won't. Imagine ringing someone's home wanting to speak to Bill or George, only to find that they're out and Rupert is the one who picks up the phone.

My experience has been that the sitter won't feel the benefit of the reading, because they will miss the information that is proffered because they're too intent on hearing from Aunty Mabel.

I also tell sitters not to have their arms crossed, legs crossed, wear dark glasses or slouch! What a hard task mistress I am.

But these situations often block energies, which is why it is obvious the information is coming from their own aura.

Chapter 7. Famous soul mate and karmic quotes

The existence of soul mates and the easy talk about Karma are not trendy new concepts. In fact poets, writers and philosophers have been talking about soul mates for years. Take a look at some of these famous quotes.

Richard Bach – American Author

"A soul mate is someone who has locks that fit our keys, and keys to fit our locks. When we feel safe enough to open the locks, our truest selves step out and we can be completely and honestly who we are; we can be loved for who we are and not for who we're pretending to be. Each unveils the best part of the other. No matter what else goes wrong around us, with that one person we're safe in our own paradise....When we're two balloons, and together our direction is up, chances are we've found the right person.

Our soul mate is the one who makes life come to life."

Kahlil Gibran - Lebanese-American author, philosopher, artist

"Know, therefore, that from the greater silence I shall return....Forget not that I shall come back to you....A little while, a moment of rest upon the wind, and another woman shall bear me."

Paul Coelho - Brazilian author, lyricist, director

"But how will I know who my soul mate is?"
"By taking risks," Wicca said to Brida. "By risking failure, disappointment, disillusion, but never ceasing in your search for Love. As long as you keep looking, you will triumph in the end."

George Eliot - British author

"What greater thing is there for two

human souls than to feel that they are joined for life? [there] to strengthen each other [and] to be at one with each other in silent unspeakable memories."

Elizabeth Gilbert - American author, journalist

"People think a soul mate is your perfect fit, and that's what everyone wants. But a true soul mate is a mirror, the person who shows you everything that is holding you back, the person who brings you to your own attention so you can change your life."

Dante Gabriel Rossetti - British poet, artist

"I have been here before, but when or how I cannot tell:

I know the grass beyond the door,

The sweet keen smell, the sighing sound, the lights around the shore.

You have been mine before - How long ago I may not know:

But just when at that swallow's soar, your neck turned so,

Some veil did fall, - I knew it all of yore."

Richard Gere American actor, humanitarian

"When someone has a strong intuitive connection, Buddhism suggests that it's because of karma, some past connection."

Plato - Ancient Greek Philosopher

"O youth or young man, who fancy that you are neglected by the gods, know that if you become worse, you shall go to worse souls, or if better to the better... In every succession of life and death, you will do and suffer what like may fitly suffer at the hands of like. This is the justice of heaven."

Yannick Noah - French Singer

"I believe in Karma. If the good is sown, the good is collected. When positive things are made, that returns well."

Sol Luckman - Author

"Contrary to popular misconceptions, karma has nothing to do with punishment and reward. It exists as part of our holographic universe's binary or dualistic operating system only to teach us responsibility for our creations - and all things we experience are our creations."

Marcia Wallace – Actress

"I don't know what religious people do. I kind of wished I'd been a Christian with the blind faith that God is doing the right thing. As a Buddhist, you feel like you have more control over the situation, and that you can change your karma."

Holly Valance - Australian Model, Actress, Singer

"I never kill insects. If I see ants or spiders in the room, I pick them up and take them outside. Karma is everything."

William Irwin Thompson - Poet and Historian

"The conscious process is reflected in the imagination; the unconscious process is expressed as karma, the generation of actions divorced from thinking and alienated from feeling."

Wayne Dyer - Speaker and Author

"How people treat you is their karma; how you react is yours."

"Begin to see yourself as a soul with a body rather than a body with a soul."

Rick Springfield - Australian Singer and Actor

"Karma is not just about the troubles, but also about surmounting them."

Tryon Edwards - Theologian

"Thoughts lead on to purposes; purposes go forth into action; actions form habits; habits decide character; and character fixes our destiny."

Sandra Bullock - Actress

"I'm a true believer in karma. You get what you give, whether it's bad or good."

Nina Hagen - German Singer

"As long as karma exists, the world changes. There will always be karma to be taken care of."

Angie Stone -Singer-Songwriter

"I would never disrespect any man, woman, chick or child out there. We're all the same. What goes around comes around, and karma kicks us all in the butt at the end of the day."

Rig Veda - Hindu Sacred Text

"The person desirous of success and strength should perform good karma continuously."

"One should perform karma with nonchalance without expecting the benefits because sooner or later one shall definitely get the fruits."

"The real happiness of life is in doing 'karma'."

"A person who performs good Karma (deeds) is always held in high esteem."

"If a householder moulds himself according to the circumstances just like nature moulds herself according to seasons and performs his Karma, then only shall he acquire happiness."

Bhagavad Gita - Hindu Sacred Text

"As the blazing fire reduces wood to ashes, similarly, the fire of self-knowledge reduces all Karma to ashes."

Sakyong Mipham Rinpoche - Shambhala Buddhist Monk and Teacher

"Karma moves in two directions. If we act virtuously, the seed we plant will result in happiness. If we act non-virtuously, suffering results."

"Like gravity, karma is so basic we often don't even notice it."

Burmese Proverb

"Worthless people blame their karma."

Tenzin Gyatso - 14th Dalai Lama

"Dangerous consequences will follow when politicians and rulers forget moral principles. Whether we believe in God or Karma, ethics is the foundation of every religion."

Sri Guru Granth Sahib - Sikh Teacher

"Without the karma of good deeds, they are only destroying themselves."

"When good karma dawns, the wall of doubt is torn down."

"According to the karma of past actions, one's destiny unfolds, even though everyone wants to be so lucky."

"Those who act in ego do not go beyond karma."

Shariyat-Ki-Sugmad - Eckankar, Book 2

"If the karma of man has brought him nothing more than a capacity to love, then he has not lived in vain for a thousand past lives. It is this love which makes the most humble of Souls so great that it lifts him beyond all life into the worlds of God."

Bodhidharma - Buddhist Monk

"Once you know the nature of anger and joy is empty and you let them go, you free yourself from karma."

"Still others commit all sorts of evil deeds, claiming karma doesn't exist. They erroneously maintain that since everything is empty, committing evil isn't wrong. Such persons fall into a hell of endless darkness with no hope of release. Those who are wise hold no such conception."

"To go from mortal to Buddha, you have to put an end to karma, nurture your awareness, and accept what life brings."

Kuan Yin - Northern Buddhist Goddess of Mercy

"There are the waves and there is the wind, seen and unseen forces. Everyone has these same elements in their lives, the seen and unseen, karma and free will."

"The thing about free will is that even if one has a huge bag of karma there is still a lot of free will for all those souls coming into the world."

Chapter 8. Famous Love Poetry

And poets have been talking about that soul mate moment for years. Here is a sample.

The First Day by Christina Rossetti

I wish I could remember the first day,
First hour, first moment of your meeting me;
If bright or dim the season it might be;
Summer or winter for aught I can say.
So, unrecorded did it slip away,
So blind was i to see and to foresee,
So dull to mark the budding of my tree
That would not blossom, yet, for many a May.

If only I could recollect it! Such
A day of days! I let it come and go
As traceless as a thaw of bygone
snow.
It seemed to mean so little, meant so
much!
If only now I could recall that touch,
First touch of hand in hand! - Did one
but know

Shall I Compare Thee, (Sonnet XVIII) by William Shakespeare

Shall I compare thee to a Summer's
day?
Thou are more lovely and more
temperate:

Rough winds do shake the darling
buds of May,

And Summer's lease hath all too short
a date:
Sometime too hot the eye of heaven
shines,
And often is his gold complexion
dimm'd;
And every fair from fair sometime
declines,
By chance or nature's changing course
untrimm'd:

But thy eternal Summer shall not fade
Nor lose possession of that fair thou
ow'st;

Nor shall Death brag thou wander'st in his shade,

When in eternal lines to time thou grow'st:
So long as men can breathe, or eyes can see,
So long lives this, and this gives life to thee.

Proud of my Broken Heart by Emily Dickinson

Proud of my broken heart, since thou didst break it.

Proud of the pain, I did not feel ?till thee.

Proud of my night, since thou, with moons, dos't shake it.

Not to partake thy passion, -my
humility

**A Friend Like You, by   Author
Unknown**

There's lots of things
With which I'm blessed,
Tho' my life's been both Sunny and
Blue,
But of all my blessings,
This one's the best:
To have a friend like you.

In times of trouble
Friends will say,
"Just ask... I'll help you through it."
But you don't wait for me to ask,
You just get up

And you do it!

And I can think

Of nothing in life

That I could more wisely do,

Than know a friend,

And be a friend,

And love a friend... like you.

A Magic Moment I Remember , by Alexander Pushkin

A magic moment I remember:

I raised my eyes and you were there.

A fleeting vision, the quintessence

Of all that's beautiful and rare.

I pray to mute despair and anguish

To vain pursuits the world esteems,

Long did I near your soothing accents,
Long did your features haunt my
dreams.

Time passed- A rebel storm-blast
scattered
The reveries that once were mine
And I forgot your soothing accents,
Your features gracefully divine.

In dark days of enforced retirement
I gazed upon grey skies above
With no ideals to inspire me,
No one to cry for, live for, love.

Then came a moment of renaissance,
I looked up- you again are there,
A fleeting vision, the quintessence

Of all that`s beautiful and rare.

How Do I Love Thee? by Elizabeth Barrett Browning

How do I love thee? Let me count the ways.
I love thee to the depth and breadth and height

My soul can reach, when feeling out of sight
For the ends of Being and ideal Grace.

I love thee to the level of everyday's
Most quiet need, by sun and candlelight.
I love thee freely, as men strive for Right;

I love thee purely, as they turn from Praise.

I love thee with the passion put to use

In my old griefs, and with my

childhood's faith.

I love thee with a love I seemed to lose

With my lost saints,--I love thee with

the breath,

Smiles, tears, of all my life!--and, if

God choose,

I shall but love thee better after death.

I Loved You, by Alexander Pushkin

I loved you-

even now I may confess

Some embers of my love their fire

retain

But do not let it cause you more
distress-
I do not want to sadden you again.

Hopeless and tongue-tied, yet, I loved
you dearly
With pangs the jealous the timid know
So tenderly I loved you, so sincerely,
I pray God grant another love you so.

Sonnet 116 by William Shakespeare

Let Me Not to the Marriage of True
Minds
Let me not to the marriage of true
minds
Admit impediments. Love is not love
Which alters when it alteration finds,

Or bends with the remover to remove:

O no! it is an ever-fixed mark

That looks on tempests and is never
shaken;

It is the star to every wandering bark,

Whose worth's unknown, although his
height be taken.

Love's not Time's fool, though rosy lips
and cheeks

Within his bending sickle's compass
come:

Love alters not with his brief hours and
weeks,

But bears it out even to the edge of
doom.

If this be error and upon me proved,

I never writ, nor no man ever loved

Chapter 9 In conclusion

So, let us return to our twin soul runner. Where did he/she go? And what were they thinking about?

In time the "runner" finds themselves in a no-brain situation. They are faced with the choice of living in pain from the separation from the Twin Soul, or returning and facing that deep love, working through their fears (often unfounded) of possible rejection and reaching their own personal Eden.

For the other party who has been willing all along to go that extra mile, the spectrum of emotions experienced till then is infinite. Sometimes they just believe that the connection is entirely one-sided, or that they've imagined it all along and feel foolish and vulnerable.

During the whole process the parties have to remain strong. Twin soul connections **never** happen at convenient times. There is often the matter of existing and committed relationships, money issues, and a whole million other practical and logical reasons why these two, on the surface shouldn't get together. There can be great differences in age, or religion or they may live continents apart.

Quite often one may be in an emotionally unfeeling, yet long term relationship, whilst the other is in a controlling and abusive one. Both can feel trapped.

But never forget, Madam Destiny in her infinite wisdom and effort has gone through the whole process and trouble of bringing these two together, and Twin Soul connections are quite rare - if you look back on this process you will inevitably come across situations where the two "nearly" met up again, or they were in the same place at the same time, and didn't meet, or they were working close to each other and didn't meet, nearly buying a house in the same town, and didn't meet, until Destiny has chosen the exact timing for that meeting and bingo, it is done.

There can be little doubt that meeting up with the Twin Soul pulls one or both onto a more spiritual path as they look back and marvel at how they were brought together.

To change one's life like this takes enormous courage, but it also takes infinite patience. And if you are in such a pairing, you can experience a Twin Soul connection both as a gift and a curse!

The lessons of why we unite with our twin soul can be varied, but one reason is to teach each other about accepting love without fear, about healing the pain of love and loss and bringing the two halves of the soul back together again.

Learning to have patience and not forcing the relationship is part of the twin soul process. If you are trying to force your will onto the other person, chances are you're not ready to really connect yourself. There should be no blame here - only deep and unconditional love.

Printed in Great Britain
by Amazon.co.uk, Ltd.,
Marston Gate.